I Went to College
and it was okay

a collection of
Jim's Journal   by **Jim**
cartoons

Andrews and McMeel
A Universal Press Syndicate Company
Kansas City

ISBN: 0-8362-1867-1

Library of Congress Catalog Card Number: 90-85798

98 99 00 01 BAH 10 9 8

I'm Jim.
This is the
journal of my
day-to-day life.

Fall Semester

Freshman Year

Today was my first day at college.

I had a big envelope filled with maps and brochures the school sent me.

Welcome!

I used them to find my way to my dorm, the cafeteria, and other places.

DIKKERS

After walking around all day I went to my dorm room and just sat there.

I met my roommate today. His name is Tony.

He came in our room and said, "Decent, decent," while he looked around.

DIKKERS

He said his brother was in college and told him all about dorms.

We could've been assigned to places a lot worse than this, Tony said.

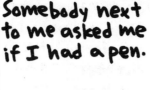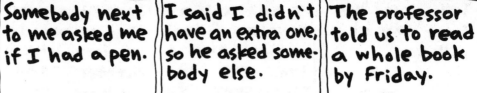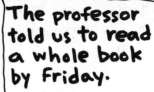

Panel 1: I went to my first class today. It was American Literature.

Panel 2: Somebody next to me asked me if I had a pen.

Panel 3: I said I didn't have an extra one, so he asked somebody else.

Panel 4: The professor told us to read a whole book by Friday.

Panel 5: I had two more classes today.

Panel 6: I'm supposed to read two or three textbook chapters for each of them.

Panel 7: Tonight Tony went down to the dorm lounge to play pool while I read.

Panel 8: I only read one and a half chapters and started getting really tired.

DIKKERS

Last night my roommate Tony stumbled in at about 2 a.m.

He threw up and then passed out.

This morning he got up and told me this is what Hell would be like.

He also said he had a pretty good time.

Yesterday in my philosophy class we learned all about Karl Marx.

It was pretty interesting.

For the rest of the day I thought about Marxism and thought it was a good philosophy.

But the next day I was back to my regular self.

| Today I slept in and missed my geology class.  | I was tired all day.  | But later I got in front of the TV.  | I had a box of Hostess Cupcakes and a bottle of Coke and I felt fine.  |

| I bought a pack of Nutter Butters yesterday.  | When I got up this morning they were all gone.  | My roommate Tony said, "I didn't know they were yours—I'll buy you another pack."  | He got me some Chips Ahoy. I guess he thinks cookies are cookies. I don't, but I like Chips Ahoy anyway. |

Yesterday I was bored.

So I took a bus to the mall.

I spent all day looking around in the book stores, record stores, and gift shops.

Today when I woke up my legs were sore.

I didn't do anything today.

I took a walk around campus last night.

I saw a couple people from one of my classes.

But they didn't recognize me.

Tony's right. He's always saying I need to get out and meet people.

I decided a job is a good way to meet some new people.

I went to McDonald's and filled out an application.

I was hired right away and a guy showed me how to put fries in their little bags.

His name was Mark or Matt or something like that.

I worked all day. I must've bagged a million fries.

I only worked a couple hours at my new job over the weekend.

But today I was back to work bagging fries.

I even learned to heat fish fillet buns.

The manager says it won't be long before I'm flipping hamburgers.

Here are some of the people I've met while working at McDonald's:

Ruth. She's always in a good mood.

Mark. He's been here 4 years and has never gotten a raise.

I think he's bitter about it.

Steve. He's the manager. He has an odd reverence for McDonald's.

I couldn't get to sleep last night.

I kept thinking I still had to bag fries.

So I watched an old movie on TV.

DIKKERS

Tony thinks I should quit my job at McDonald's.

But I kinda like it.

I stayed home all day today.

I think I'm coming down with a cold.

DIKKERS

My throat is sore. I hate that.

I think sore throats are the worst thing there is.

I knew it. I have a cold.

I look like this.

But I feel like this.

I hate colds.

I've been taking a lot of cold medicine.

I feel like a giant bottle of Liquid Comtrex.

That stuff tastes terrible.

And it only makes me feel better for a couple hours.

There's only one good thing about having a cold.

It makes you appreciate when you're healthy.

I was feeling a lot better today. I went to work and school.

When I got home, Tony was coughing and sniffling. It looks like he has a cold now.

I ran into Ruth today. She works at McDonald's with me.

She looked different out of uniform.

We'd never talked outside of work before.

We didn't seem to know what to say to each other.

Last night I went to a movie with Tony and his friends.

It was pretty good.

Today at McDonald's I learned to work the cash register.

I was really slow—too many buttons to remember.

Customers probably thought I was sort of stupid.

I felt sort of stupid for the rest of the day.

I had a test in my geology class today.	Before class everybody was going over notes and quizzing each other.	I got a little nervous because I didn't know half of what they were talking about.	But the test wasn't so bad, and I think I did okay.

Tony came into McDonald's today.	I'm not sure why, but I was embarrassed when I saw him.	He said I looked like an organ grinder's monkey, and that didn't help.	Incidentally, Tony ordered a Big Mac, fries, and a Coke.

(that's what everybody orders)

DIKKERS

I crammed for a test all morning.

Then I took the test.

I could've done a lot better.

I have another test tomorrow, but I can study for it in the morning.

I had a lot of tests this week... My brain is exhausted.

On my way home today I saw a guy playing his saxophone on the sidewalk.

I sat and listened to him.

It was just what I needed.

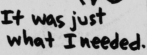

Last night I was sitting around when I thought of how good a pizza would taste.	I called to have one delivered, but it never came.	I called again and they said it would be late, but with $2 off.	It came a half hour later. It was practically cold.
			 I should've made a peanut-butter sandwich.

I spent most of my day in the library.	I was there to read "The Sound and the Fury" for my literature class.	Then I came home and watched TV.	TV seemed a lot more stupid than it usually does.

DIKKERS

All I could think about today was sleep.

I stayed up till 6am. last night writing a paper.

I forgot about it till the last minute.

It's probably the worst paper I've ever written.

I got a B on that paper I wrote the other night.

Maybe I should write all my papers in a last minute rush.

I think they come out better that way.

Today I bought some of those strawberry Newtons.

They were pretty good.

I went home for Thanksgiving.

I ate a lot and saw a lot of relatives that I hadn't seen in a while.

I hung around with my hometown friends too.

DIKKERS

But that wasn't quite like it used to be.

Today Tony asked me to write a paper for him.

I refused, but he kept asking me.

"It's the principle of the thing," I kept saying.

DIKKERS

I actually considered doing it when he offered me $50.

But I have enough of my own work to do.

Tony's term paper was due today.

Yesterday I told him I wouldn't write it for him—even though he said he'd pay me.

So he stayed up late writing it himself, occasionally asking for my help.

DIKKERS

This morning, before he woke up, I read it.

I felt sorry for him. It was pretty bad.

I got up late today.

I tried to get to my first class on time.

But while walking to it I realized I'd already missed half of it, so I decided not to go.

DIKKERS

The rest of the day seemed to go by in no time.

I felt like doing something different today.

So I walked by the lake.

DIKKERS

I almost froze after only a few minutes.

I went to the bookstore instead.

I just browsed, like I always do.

A guy came into McDonald's today and didn't order any food.

He just asked for a handful of ketchup.

He comes in a lot.

DIKKERS

He probably saves a lot of money on ketchup.

I have my final exams this week. 	I took one this morning. It wasn't too bad. 	I came home and ate some doughnuts and watched TV. 	Tony told me he has two final exams at the same time tomorrow. 
I went back to my hometown today. 	My mom said, "Hi, Jim." 	She said Miles Fikema got married, and I didn't know what she was talking about. 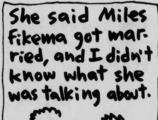	Then I remembered that the Fikemas were one of our neighbors. 

DIKKERS

Today I slept till noon.

I got up and looked out the window.

DIKKERS

I went downstairs to make some breakfast. My mom had a lot of food.

My grandma visited today from Oregon.

She brought presents and fudge.

I ate so much fudge that I didn't feel like eating anything else all day.

DIKKERS

My grandma asked me all about what I was taking in school.

Today was New Year's Day. 	Tony called me. 	"Hey, happy New Year, Jim!" he said. 	He told me all about what he did to celebrate last night. 
It's nice not having any home-work to do. 	It snowed today. 	My mom said she liked having me around so I could shovel the driveway. 	Even though it was cold, I got so warm shoveling that I took my coat off. 

DIKKERS

Spring Semester

Freshman Year

I came back to school today.

I watched TV all day.

Later at night I went to the grocery store... I felt like a zombie.

EXPRES LANE
12 ITEMS OR LESS

I have a class with Mark, who works at McDonald's with me.

I feel uneasy around Mark.

He always points out the dreary, hopeless aspect of everything.

I think he just does it to be funny, but I'm not sure.

DIKKERS

I had a shake-spearean drama class today.

I came late & forgot my book and notebook.

I borrowed a pen from somebody and took notes on the back of my syllabus.

When I got home I couldn't find the notes I took.

Tony started a new weight-lifting regime last night.

It was peaceful while he was at the gym.

I got a lot of reading done.

When he came back he said he lifted weights for 2½ hours and felt great.

This morning he could barely move.

I don't think he even went to his classes today.

Today I went to class, worked at McDonald's, etc...

It was an average day.

Tony was feeling well enough today to hobble to class.

He says he'll never lift weights again.

After my classes today I started a story for my creative-writing class.

The story isn't due till next Wednesday, but I had an idea for it today.

It's a science-fiction story in which everything in the universe disappears.

But I can't think of where to take it from there.

A couple of guys asked for job applications at McDonald's today.

They laughed hysterically while they filled them out.

They used silly pseudonyms and wrote "Pope" for previous employment and things like that.

Steve, the manager, was angry. He threw the applications away.

I thought they were pretty funny.

At work today I spent most of my time mopping the floor.

I didn't think I'd exerted myself very much,

but when I got home I was exhausted.

I ran into Sam today. He works at McDonald's.

He wanted me to work for him tomorrow night.

I told him I couldn't because I was already working then.

DIKKERS

I felt sorry for him. He said he'd miss a quiz if he had to work.

I did my laundry today.

There are washers and dryers in the basement of where I live.

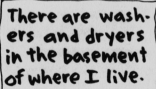

Somebody else was finishing up a load while I waited for mine.

DIKKERS

He took his clothes out of the dryer and folded them really neatly.

I felt like doing something different today.

So I got on a bus and went around the route a couple times.

All the bumping around made me tired.

DIKKERS

I wasn't in the mood to be in school today.

The professors might as well've been reading the phone book to me.

I just wasn't interested.

DIKKERS

I came home and took a nap—something I hardly ever do.

When I got up I felt energetic and creative.

I stayed up till 3 am. reading Trivial Pursuit answers.

Today in my writing class Mark read his story aloud.

Everyone thought it needed some revising.

Mark told me later that he'd been working on his story for months...

...that every word had been chosen with extreme care. It couldn't be revised, he said.

DIKKERS

I sit behind someone in philosophy class who pretends to be taking notes.

But she's actually writing a letter to her friend... I can see it.

DIKKERS

Once she even raised her hand and asked a question.

But then she went right back to writing her letter.

Today I sat by the window in a restaurant all morning.

I watched all the people walk by.

It was my room-mate Tony's birthday today.

He said he would celebrate like a madman tonight.

I had to stay late at the library to study for a test.

But on my way home I walked by a bar and saw Tony in there.

He was just sitting there, alone.

DIKKERS

Tony was his usual self today.	He said none of his friends were available for his birthday party last night.	But all of them promised to do something with him this weekend.	He said he will celebrate like a madman this weekend.

I woke up at 4:30 this morning and couldn't get back to sleep.	So I went outside and walked around.	It was peaceful, but strange without all the people.	After a while I went back home and slept till noon.

As I was leaving for the grocery store today, Tony asked me to get him some CoolWhip.

But I forgot to get some.

The strange thing is, Tony never said anything about it.

DIKKERS

I guess he forgot too.

Today I showed up an hour early for my philosophy class and read the newspaper

After a few minutes I'd read everything interesting in it.

So I read beyond the assigned chapters in my philosophy textbook.

DIKKERS

It felt good to be ahead in the readings.

My roommate Tony and his friends left for Florida today for spring break.

They're driving an old Volkswagen Bug that sounds like a tractor.

Its headlights are held in place with long strips of duct tape.

"I'd crawl to Florida if I had to," Tony said before he left.

I rode my bike as far out of town as I could today.

No reason, really. It was just something to do.

The countryside was a pleasant change of scenery, and I got a lot of exercise.

I should probably do things like that more often.

DIKKERS

| I didn't feel like watching TV today. | There was nothing on anyway. | I decided to do some homework instead. | But I didn't feel like doing homework either. |

| Today in creative-writing class our stories were returned to us, graded. | Mark got a C. | He stayed after class to complain about his grade to the professor. | Later, Mark told me he didn't believe artistic expression should be graded. |

| My roommate Tony bought a little tape recorder the other day. | He's decided to tape his classes from now on. | Today I went to the music department. | I sat and read a book while listening to people practice their instruments. |

| Tony has been sitting around watching TV a lot lately— | even more than I usually do, which is quite a bit. | He says it's okay that he's not doing any homework because he has all his classes on tape. | He says he has all weekend to catch up. |

Today Mark said he and his friends would be watching a movie on his VCR tonight.

He said the movie would be Dawn of the Dead, his favorite. He said I was invited.

So I went.

Mark & his friends had a lot of the lines memorized and were laughing so much that I couldn't hear the movie.

We had an employee's meeting at McDonald's today.

DIKKERS

Everybody was there—even some people I'd never seen before.

Steve, the manager, talked about the good job we've been doing, and how we could improve.

He seemed uncomfortable talking to all those people.

Tony's been taping his classes regularly.

But it seems like he never listens to the tapes — they keep piling up.

Today I borrowed his tape player.

I was going to take a walk and listen to one of my favorite tapes.

But my tape had been erased. It had one of Tony's lectures on it

I stayed up late last night watching TV.

So I was tired today.

In my creative-writing class, Mark was talking to me.

But I was so tired that I wasn't even listening to him.

Tony had a big test today.

He spent most of yesterday catching up on listening to the lectures he taped.

He told me today that he doesn't think he failed the test.

He said taping classes is a pretty good idea.

Tony's parents came to visit for a few days.

They seemed nice.

Tony was embarrassed by almost everything they said and did.

"So you're Tony's roommate," they said to me.

Tony's parents are still here.

They're staying in a hotel a few blocks away.

But they spend most of their time being shown around the campus by Tony.

Today Tony's dad asked me all about my classes, where I was from, my career plans, and so on.

But I couldn't think of anything to ask about him.

Tony's parents left today.

After he came home from his classes, Tony talked to me for a while.

He told me all the little things about his parents that bothered him.

They seemed like okay parents to me.

Today I walked to McDonald's with Ruth, who works there with me.

She told me about her goal of becoming a dental technician.

I made hamburgers, fish fillets and chicken nuggets at McDonald's.

Then I went home.

Today I washed the windows at McDonald's.

I liked it.

I didn't have to pay attention to anything else around me.

I just washed the windows.

DIKKERS

Today Mark didn't come to creative-writing class.

The class was quiet without him.

Later in the day I was watching TV while eating some fish sticks.

I wondered why Mark hadn't come to class.

I was sitting around today reading when Tony called.

He said he forgot his notes for an open-notebook test and wanted me to bring them to him.

I said I would.

I wasn't at all inconvenienced by bringing Tony his notes, but he thanked me as if I'd crawled 300 miles to bring them.

For the rest of the day I felt like I'd done a really good deed.

It was a busy day at McDonald's today. (I was making fries.)

When I came home Tony was watching The Brady Bunch on TV.

"Look at those pants Marsha's wearing!" he said, laughing.

It was kind of funny, but I didn't feel like watching the whole show.

I got my phone bill today.

I didn't realize I'd made so many long-distance calls.

From now on I'll write down every long-distance call I make.

And I won't make a long-distance call unless I absolutely have to.

Today I had my Shakespearean drama class.	Before class, the person next to me was talking to me.	She said she hated Shakespeare, but is getting a B anyway.	She said she usually gets B's.

Last night I couldn't get to sleep.	The people next door were having a loud party.	This morning I could barely stay awake.	And my roommate Tony told me all about the neighbors' party.

Today at McDonald's I accidentally dropped a tray of hamburgers.

Steve, the manager, didn't say anything about it.

I cleaned up the mess, then continued making hamburgers.

Actually, Steve didn't talk to me all day after I dropped the hamburgers.

I've decided to go back to my home town for the summer.

DIKKERS

Today I told Steve, the manager at McDonald's, that I'll be quitting.

He asked if I expected to be rehired after the summer.

I said "not really."

I'd like to work at some place other than McDonald's in the fall.

I studied for my final exams while sitting outside today.

Tony was sitting outside too.

I also saw Sam, from McDonald's.

I told him I'd quit at McDonald's. He said he plans to stay there all summer.

Today I walked by Steve on the sidewalk.

I didn't know he had a baby.

Steve noticed me but he didn't say anything.

I guess I'll probably never see him again.

DIKKERS

Summer

I came back to my hometown today.

I talked to my mom for a while.

She wanted to know what I was going to do all summer.

I said I didn't want to do much of anything.

Today my mom left for work in the morning.

(She's a piano teacher.)

I sat around at home.

I read a short story in the Atlantic Monthly today.

(My mom has a subscription.)

It was okay.

I thought maybe I should write a story, since I didn't have much else to do.

But I didn't really feel like it.

My high-school friend Sue came to visit today.

She's home from college for the summer too.

She told me about one of her professors who she said was really eccentric.

She described him and laughed, I could imagine him being pretty funny.

I went for a bike ride today.

I stopped at a gas station and bought a can of Coke.

I sat on the curb and drank it.

DIKKERS

It was nice and cold at first, but then it tasted like syrup.

I was bored today.

I went outside and walked around.

I walked by a guy washing his car. A suntan lotion ad was playing on his radio.

When I got home I tried to figure out the notes to the suntan lotion theme on the piano.

Today my high-school friend Dave came over.

He said he and some of our other friends from high school were going to a movie tonight.

He wanted to know if I wanted to come.

I said I would.

DIKKERS

I went to a movie last night with Dave and his friends.

Afterwards we went to Hardee's and Gene squashed ketchup packets with his fist.

Dave and the rest of them laughed and people looked at us like we were crazy.

DIKKERS

I had an okay time, but I was glad to get home.

I've been sleep-
ing in late all
summer.

Today I got
up at 1:30.

After a while
my mom came
home from work.

"Did you just get
up?" she said.

She couldn't
believe I slept
so late.

I went to see
my dad today.

He lives just
across the state
line from my
mom.

They got divorced
a long time ago.

"Well look who's
here," he said.

I rode my bike around today.

I went past my high school.

I walked through it and it looked pretty much the same as I remember it.

There were some guys from the high-school football team training outside.

Today I went to visit my friend Sue.

She answered the door and said, "Hi, Jim," then ran back into her house.

I heard her tell me to come in, so I did.

She was watching a soap opera, and told me what was happening on it.

I slept in till 2:00 today.

I ate a bowl of cereal and watched some game shows on TV.

When my mom came home from work I was still sitting around.

"You look like you need something to do," she said.

My mom asked me to mow the lawn today.

It doesn't seem like a big yard, but it took me a long time.

Today one of my high-school teachers came to our house.

She's a friend of my mom.

She wanted to know all about what I thought of college.

But I couldn't think of anything to say about it.

I went to the grocery store today.

My mom sent me with a list of things to buy.

As I was leaving with the groceries, the cashier ran up to me.

"You forgot your receipt," she said.

I visited my dad again today.

He was painting his garage, and I helped.

"The old paint was peeling like crazy," he said.

He told me his neighbors just painted their house and garage.

My friend Dave came by today.

He said he was going to another movie tonight with his friends.

I told him I didn't really feel like coming along.

He said, "Come on, it'll be a great time!"

Last night Dave and my other friends stopped by.

They were on their way to a movie.

Dave asked me to come. I said I felt like staying home.

"You don't want to go out with your ol' high-school pals?" he said.

I guess I just didn't.

When I got up today I saw a note from my mom.

She wanted me to wash a load of clothes.

So I did.

While the washer and dryer were going I looked through my old stuff, which my mom stores in the basement.

Sue came over today.	We sat around and talked.	We agreed that summer can get boring, but it's a nice break from college.	"I can't wait to get out of school and get a job," she said.
			(She wants to go into advertising.)

Today I took a walk.	I stopped at Dairy Queen and had a peanut buster parfait.	I sat outside.	I watched an ant, who was walking across the table in a roundabout way.

Fall
Semester

Sophomore
Year

I live in a new apartment with my old roommate Tony, and a new roommate, Steve.

DIKKERS

Tony was angry when he found out that the intercom didn't work.

He got even more angry when he found out that we didn't have a cable TV hookup.

He says our new apartment is a dump, but other than that I think it's an OK place.

This is Tony's and my new roommate, Steve.

Steve went to the same high school Tony did, but was one grade behind Tony.

DIKKERS

Today Tony said Steve doesn't get any space in the refrigerator 'cause he's a freshman.

He was just kidding.

Steve (Tony's and my new roommate) went to the same high school as Tony.

Tony was sitting around today reminiscing about people he remembered from high school.

He was throwing out names and laughing uproariously, asking Steve if he remembered them.

Steve only knew of one or two. I don't think Steve and Tony had the same friends in high school.

I went to class today.

The person next to me had a new notebook, a new folder, freshly sharpened pencils, and a new 3-ring binder.

She wrote her name, the name of the class, and the name of the professor at the top of a piece of paper.

But she didn't write anything else for the rest of the hour.

I got up early today.

Before class I went to the store to buy some breakfast.

Then I went to my first class, which is U.S. history.

Today I was woken up by a loud crunching sound

There was also the sound of the TV.

Steve was watching Good Morning America and eating Froot Loops right out of the box.

I got up early again today.	I was about to leave for class when Tony woke up.	Steve was watching Good Morning America and eating Froot Loops right out of the box.	"How can you eat those without milk?" Tony asked.

I had my U.S. history class today.	We learned about what life was like in the new-world colonies.	I was taking notes, like I usually do.	The person next to me looked at my notes and wrote everything that I wrote.

I went to my U.S. history class today.

When I came home I felt like reading a little bit of my U.S. history book.

But I realized I had all weekend to read it so I watched TV.

After a while Tony came home, ran into his room, then left in a hurry.

After class today I went to work at McDonald's.

Last time I worked there was 4 or 5 months ago.

I'd forgotten how much hard work it is.

(I worked from 2:30 till 6.)

DIKKERS

| When I came home from work today I sat and watched TV with Steve.  | I told him I'd just come back from McDonald's.  | He was surprised. He didn't know I worked there.  | He said he'd have to come in and eat when I'm working some time.  |

| I ran into Tony on campus today.  | He didn't say much except that he needed to borrow a quarter.  | I said I didn't have one and he said "Damn it, I'll see ya later, Jim."  | I felt pretty bad later when I found a quarter in my pocket.  |

Mike is a guy who usually works at McDonald's when I'm there.

Today he was squashing old hamburgers in the trash compactor.

He said college can't give you hands-on experience like this.

It was pretty funny.

Cheryl, the manager, thought it was funny too, but she told us to get back to work.

Last night Tony was watching TV with a friend.

I did some homework in my room.

A while later, I went to the kitchen to get a sandwich.

"I'm a pretty sensitive guy," I heard Tony tell his friend.

This morning Tony said "Hey, whadjya think of Karen?"

He was talking about his friend from last night.

I said I didn't meet her or anything, but guessed she was pretty nice.

"'Pretty nice?' She's the hottest chick in town!" he said.

Today Steve was talking to me about Tony's girlfriend.

"Why do you s'pose she likes Tony?" he said.

Then Tony came Home... After that we didn't say much.

"Guess who's got a hot date tonight, gentlemen!" Tony said.

After my psychology class today I didn't go home right away.

I wandered around the psychology building and read all the cartoons on the office doors.

Some of them were pretty funny.

They were all cartoons about psychology.

DIKKERS

This morning I got up early to study for a U.S. history test.

But I didn't feel like studying, so I watched TV.

After a while, Steve got up and watched TV too.

He asked me if I'd mind turning the channel to Good Morning America.

So I did.

DIKKERS

I worked late at McDonald's today.

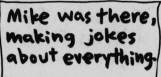

Mike was there, making jokes about everything.

But I wasn't really in the mood to laugh.

After a while my mouth was tired from pretending to smile, and I just wanted to go home.

Today I was working at McDonald's during lunch.

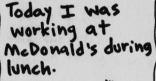

My roommate Steve came in and said hello.

Then he ordered a Big Mac with no special sauce, no pickles, and double the lettuce.

He also told me not to toast the bun.

Today Tony's friend (who has a car) drove us to the grocery store.	Steve and I sat in the back seat.	Tony sat in front with his friend, laughing, talking and playing tapes.	We spent a lot of money and got a lot of food.

The phone was ringing today when I came home.	Whoever it was hung up before I answered it.	I thought they might call back later.	But the phone didn't ring for the rest of the day.

Today I went to my psychology class. 	The professor wrote on an overhead projector. 	It wasn't focused very well, and I had trouble seeing what she was writing. 	All the lights were off too, and I got really sleepy. 
Today after my U.S. history class I went to eat a taco. 	I read some of my U.S. history text book while I ate. 	It was pretty interesting. 	I should probably read my text books more often. 

Today I didn't feel like getting out of bed.

I don't know why. I just didn't.

Then Tony came into my room and said, "Hey, you bum, get up! There's a phone call for you!"

It was Ruth from McDonald's. She wanted me to work for her today.

I said I would.

Today I went to my psychology class.

Then I went to the store and bought a candy bar.

I guess it's been a while since I've eaten one.

It didn't taste as good as I remember.

Today was a pretty typical day.

I was sitting around this afternoon watching TV. (So was Steve.)

A police car with its siren going drove by outside.

"They finally caught you, Jim," Steve said.

Today at McDonald's they started an evaluation of the employees.

While I was flipping hamburgers, Cheryl, the manager, watched me.

Today I got a letter from an old high-school friend.

As I was reading it I felt like writing back.

I thought of all the things I could write about.

But later, I didn't feel like writing back at all.

Today my psychology class seemed longer than usual.

I kept looking at the clock, and it didn't seem to be moving very fast.

When the class finally ended I was really tired.

So I went home and took a nap.

Today Steve was sifting through all his belongings.

"I brought too much stuff when I moved here!" he said.

I looked through his high-school year book.

I found his picture and it looked kind of funny.

Today Steve decided to get rid of the stuff he didn't need.

He asked me if I wanted his Humphrey Bogart poster.

I said I didn't.

Today Steve cleaned his room.	He vacuumed it and everything.	When he was done, Tony and I looked at it.	It was pretty clean.

I worked until closing time tonight at McDonald's.	I didn't go home right away.	I walked on the train tracks next to the campus.	It was really quiet, except for cars going by now and then.

Today Steve came home while I was making a sand- wich.

"I don't think college is for me," he said.

Then Tony came home and said, "Women! I just can't figure 'em!"

We sat around in the kitchen and talked about our problems for quite a while.

I was working at McDonald's today when Tony's girlfriend Karen came in (with a friend).

"Hey, you're Tony's roommate," she said.

"Tony...God, what a jerk," her friend said.

They laughed, even though they were trying not to.

They ordered two ice cream cones.

I was just sitting around today when Tony came home.

"She never wants to do anything with me anymore, I swear!" he said.

He talked about it for almost an hour, but not really to me.

He made light of it, but I think he was actually pretty sad.

Today Steve rented a movie on video.

It was Star Trek II: The Wrath of Khan.

I didn't really feel like watching it because I had homework to do.

But I ended up watching the whole thing anyway.

We had a test today in my U.S. history class.	Lately I haven't been studying as much as I should.	I had trouble thinking of the answers.	

In my psychology class today we had to get in little groups.	We were supposed to think up an undesired behavior.	Nobody in my group knew each other, so it was kind of awkward at first.	Eventually we decided on finger-nail biting.

I went to my U.S. history class today.

I read the assigned chapters in the text book beforehand.

I felt bad about not studying for the test the other day.

So I decided to try harder this time.

Today at McDonald's we found out the results of our employee evaluations.

Ruth was promoted to crew chief. (She's worked here a long time.)

I got a 10¢-per-hour raise.

So did Mike.

I got up late today to the sound of music I'd never heard before.

It was loud.

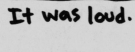

Tony was dancing to it in the hall.

He said it was a tape of Eskimo song duels that he had to listen to for his music appreciation class.

Today when I came home from school Tony was watching TV and playing a tape.

I recognized the music. I looked at the tape. It was The Blue Danube.

Tony said he was listening to it for his music appreciation class.

He said it was too boring to listen to by itself, which is why he was watching TV.

"Jim," Tony said today, "if you ever see a record by John Cage, I strongly recommend you don't buy it."

I asked him why he was listening to all this music so late in the semester.

He told me it was because the test wasn't until today.

"I don't know why I ever took this class," he said.

Today I worked at McDonald's flipping hamburgers.

Mike was working on the cash register.

The radio was on and I was getting sick of hearing the same songs over and over.

Once Mike said, "Hey, somebody just ordered a hamburger without the bun!"

DIKKERS

Last night Tony and Steve and I watched "How The Grinch Stole Christmas" on TV.

Steve said he always watched shows like The Grinch every Christmas when he was a kid.

Tony said they shouldn't show it on TV so early. "It's November!" he said.

But he said he used to watch it every year too.

There's a 6-page paper due in my psychology class in two days.

Actually, it's an optional paper, but I'd like to do it because it will help my grade.

The trouble is, I can't think of a topic.

DIKKERS

I'm behind in my classes, so I need to do a lot of work to catch up.

Last night I was doing some homework, but it gave me a headache.

I walked around outside awhile to get some fresh air.

But it didn't help. My head still ached, and I felt even less like doing homework than before.

I went to see a movie last night.

tickets

I came home and told Tony I saw a movie and he said, "You saw a movie all by yourself?!"

Today I went to my psychology class.

When it was over, a guy sitting next to me said, "So, are you ready for the final exam?"

I'd never seen or talked to him before, but he was really friendly.

He said, "I'm not... It's gonna be a couple all-nighters for me," then he laughed.

I didn't have any food today so I went to the grocery store.

Steve said he needed some food too, so he came along.

On the way there, Steve said, "I hate this weather. It's too cold."

Today I went to my psychology class

When I came home, Tony was studying for his finals.

So was Steve.

Today I worked at McDonald's.

Ruth was there.

She said the employees are having a Christmas party and I'm invited.

I said I'd come.

DIKKERS

There were a lot of people at the McDonald's Christmas party today, all laughing and talking.

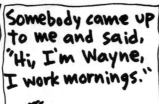

Somebody came up to me and said, "Hi, I'm Wayne, I work mornings."

Cheryl, the manager, talked to me for a while.

I felt awkward talking to her. I'm used to just doing what she says.

DIKKERS

I had a final exam today.

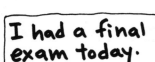

I studied for it all last night.

DIKKERS

The test had three different essay questions and I had to pick one.

Two of them I didn't know much about, but luckily one of them was pretty easy.

Steve and Tony left for winter break today.

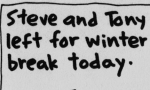

They both live in Hudson, Wisconsin, so they rode there together.

Steve asked me if I could think of anything he could get his parents for Christmas.

"We'll find something on the way there," Tony said. "Let's go!"

It's quiet without Steve and Tony around.

Hardly anybody comes into McDonald's because everybody on campus went home.

My grandma sent me a pair of socks and a Christmas card today.

Spring Semester

Sophomore
Year

Today I got some of the books I'll need for my classes.

They cost a lot.

Some of them looked like they'd be fun to read.

But I probably won't want to read them when they're assigned.

Today I had an astronomy class.

The professor used up the whole class reading the syllabus to us.

Today I had a Chinese history class.

Then I came home and read the first few chapters in the text book.

Today I worked at McDonald's.

During my break, Ruth was telling me what it was like to be crew chief.

"Being crew chief isn't much different than being one of the crew people," she said.

She finished her cup of Coke and started chewing on the ice cubes.

Today when I woke up, Tony was leaving for an 8 o'clock class.

"Top o' the mornin' to ya, Jim," he said.

He smelled like cologne.

After he left, I had a bowl of cheerios, and I could still smell the cologne.

My astronomy class made me think today.

I saw the earth as just a tiny speck floating in space.

I came home and Steve was watching "Win Lose or Draw."

I asked him if he ever thought of how insignificant we all are.

He said he has.

I was bored today.
I flipped around some radio stations for a while...
I went to the bookstore and browsed...
When the day was over, I was amazed at how I'd frittered it away.
DIKKERS

I had my Chinese history class today.
DIKKERS
I was looking at my desk.
It had political platitudes etched in it...
U.S. out of Central America
Just say No to Apartheid
and the names of a couple rock bands too.
U2
Guns -N- Roses

Today Tony and I were watching TV and eating.

We heard something get thrown against the wall in Steve's room.

Then Steve stomped out the door and slammed it.

Today I went to a movie with Sam and Ruth, from McDonald's.

Right at the plot climax, the picture went blank, and we just had the sound.

Then they rewound the film and showed the end again, with a picture.

But it wasn't very good because we already had a pretty good idea what happened.

Today after class I ran into Mark.	He used to work at McDonald's.	He was in one of my classes last year too.	He said he hasn't been up to much.

Today I was going to the grocery store. (I was all out of cereal.)	I asked Steve if he wanted to come.	He said he had too much homework to do.	But he didn't look like he wanted to do his homework at all.

DIKKERS

At McDonald's today Mike was making fries.	He accidentally dropped the fry rack and got splattered with boiling grease.	His arm had dark red spots on it where the grease hit it.	Cheryl, the manager, put some medication on it.

Mike came to work today.	He had a big bandage on his arm from his burn yesterday.	Once his arm almost touched the Big Mac bun toaster plate (which is really hot).	We couldn't believe the bad luck of almost getting burned in the same place twice.

Today Steve and I were just sitting around.

Tony sat down with a plate of Spaghettios.

"You know what this place needs?" he said...."A sofa."

"This place definitely needs a sofa," he said.

When I got up today, Tony was looking through the newspaper.

He was pointing out all the ads for furniture.

(He wants to buy a sofa.)

Later, I went to my Chinese History class.

We read Confucius' Analects.

Steve was writing a book report today.

He said it was easy in high school— you just had to write a summary.

DIKKERS

"How are you supposed to know how to do a college book report?" he said.

Tony bought a sofa today.

DIKKERS

He bought it from his friend Kurt, who helped him move it.

"20 bucks. You can't beat that." Tony said.

After a while we all sat in it and he said, "what do you think, guys?"

I went to the library this morning to read my Chinese history book.	But I didn't feel like reading, so I just doodled in my notebook.	Tony had a couple friends over today.	They were just sitting around talking.
Today I went to my astronomy class.	On my way home I saw Steve.	He had just bought some batteries.	

This morning my clock-radio went off, but I didn't feel like getting up.

I listened to the radio for almost an hour.

It was on an all-news station, which had a lot of commercials.

I heard one commercial three times. (It was for Therapeutic Mineral Ice.)

Today I accidentally cut my thumb on a piece of paper.

"Ooh, a paper cut, those are the worst!" Tony said

But it wasn't too bad.

I tried to put on a Band-Aid, but it was hard to open.

The red string just came right out, and I had to tear the little package all up.

Today I got a call from Cheryl, the manager at McDonald's.

She told me I was late for work.

I went there, but I was pretty sure I wasn't supposed to work today.

I looked at the schedule, and it had my name on it for today.

Today Steve came home when Tony and I were sitting around watching TV.

"I've had it. I'm quitting school," he said.

"I'm just not smart enough for college," he said. He was angry.

"Come on," Tony said. "Nobody just up and quits school!"

"What would you do if you quit school?" Tony asked Steve this morning.

"I'll get a job or something," Steve said.

"You're gunna work at McDonald's, like Jim? For the rest of your life?!" Tony said.

"A college degree is your ticket to a decent job," he said.

This morning I was reading the newspaper.

When I was done, Tony took it. "I gotta read my horoscope," he said.

"Damn!" he said.

Today Steve and I were sitting around watching TV. 	Steve said. "Jim, do you think I should quit school?" 	I said, "I don't know."	
Today I got up late and skipped my astronomy class. 	Later at night I worked at McDonald's.  Ruth was there.	She had an interview with a dentist today and thought she did pretty well. 	Ruth wants to be a dental technician. 

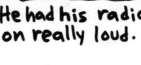
Today Tony was cleaning the bathroom.

He had his radio on really loud.

I was trying to read my astronomy book, but I couldn't concentrate.

So I listened to the radio.

On my way home from class today I bought a scrub brush.

Tony said we needed one, and asked me if I'd pick one up.

I came home and gave it to him.

"Thanks, Jim," he said. "Now stay out of the kitchen for a while."

(He was cleaning the kitchen.)

I got my bike out today.

I haven't ridden it since September.

Almost everything on it needed to get fixed.

I couldn't figure out how to fix it so I took it to a bike shop.

OIKKERS

It should be fixed in a couple days, the guy said.

Steve came back from spring break yesterday.

He brought a kitten with him from his parents' farm.

DIKKERS

"I named him Mr. Peterson," Steve said.

Mr. Peterson looked like he was afraid of all of us.

Mr. Peterson, the cat Steve brought home, was hiding in a corner today.

"Come here, Mr. Peterson. Come here, Mr. Peterson," Tony said.

But Mr. Peterson stayed in the corner.

Tony told Steve he should have gotten a dog.

I have to write a paper for my chinese history class.

But I can't think of a topic.

Today I was sitting in the kitchen, eating a bowl of soup.

Steve came in and said, "I'm hungry, but I can't think of anything to eat."

Today Steve and I were watching TV.

"College isn't for me, but I'm going to stick it out for the semester," Steve said.

I asked him what he would do when he left school.

DIKKERS

He said he'd go back to his hometown and get a job.

Today in my astronomy class we learned about astrology.

The professor said the Earth's position's changed since ancient times, when astrology started.

So the zodiac signs don't match the constellations they're named after.

DIKKERS

He said that's why even if astrology worked, horoscopes would be wrong.

 I went to talk to my Chinese-history professor today.

 I told him I can't think of a topic for my paper.

 He made a lot of suggestions. They all sounded pretty good.

 But a little later I still didn't know what to write about.

 Today I was eating a peanut-butter and jelly sandwich.

 Mr. Peterson looked at me and meowed over and over.

meow meow

 It seemed like he really wanted something from me.

meow

 But I didn't know what he wanted, so I couldn't help him.

meow meow

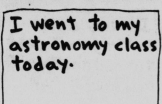 I went to my astronomy class today.

 Then I came home and ate a tuna sandwich and watched Jeopardy on TV.

 Then I worked at McDonald's.

 When it was almost closing time, Cheryl said, "It's been a long day."

 I still haven't written a chinese history paper. I don't have a topic.

 Today in class we looked at pictures of pottery from the T'ang Dynasty.

 Someone sitting behind me said, "Some of these pots are just outrageous!"

 So I decided pottery would be a pretty good topic.

I went to the library again today.

I'm still look-ing through books to research my term paper.

I felt like going home and taking a nap.

One time I looked at a page in my book and saw the words as just a big gray blob.

I finished my Chinese-history paper over the weekend.

It turned out okay. I hope I never have to write another one.

Today Tony said, "Hey, Jim, think of a topic for my poli-sci term paper."

I told him I didn't want to think about term papers anymore.

Ruth was working at McDonald's today.

She was talking to me about the weather.

She said she likes winter because she grew up in the North.

But she said she's happy that it's warming up.

I accidentally left my jacket at McDonald's yesterday.

Ruth brought it to me on her way home from work today.

"She's huge!" Tony said.

Today Steve said, "Jim, did you ever read The Prince by Machiavelli?"

I told him I was pretty sure I had.

"It's pretty interesting," he said.

"Is that a tuna sandwich?" he asked. I said it was.

Today Tony, Steve and I watched The Music Man on TV.

Tony said his high school put on the play and he had two or three lines.

He was waiting to see the part he played.

Finally he said, "There! that was me!" And he tried to say the lines along with the scene.

Today at McDonald's Mike and I had to clean the walk-in refrigerator.

We took all the boxes of ketchup, shake mix and stuff down stairs. It took a long time.

After a while Mike stopped. He was breathing hard.

"I don't think this is my calling, Jim." he said.

Tony and I were watching TV Today.

Tony was eating a couple hot dogs, and Mr. Peterson wanted some.

"Doesn't Steve ever feed his cat?" Tony said.

I said I was pretty sure Steve fed him.

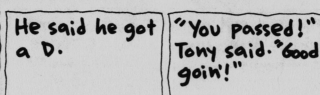

| Today Steve came home from school with a test he got back, graded. | He said he got a D. | "You passed!" Tony said. "Good goin'!" | Steve said he's been trying really hard. "I don't know why I bother," he said. |

| Tony was studying for a test today. | "I'll never learn all this by tomorrow!" he said. | Then Steve told Tony that cramming isn't the best way to study. | "Look who's talking," Tony said. "Albert Einstein in the flesh." |

DIKKERS

DIKKERS

Mr. Peterson woke me up today.

He was sitting on me kneading his paws.

I got up and noticed Steve and Tony were gone, and Mr. Peterson's food bowl was empty.

I put some food in it and he ate it.

Today at McDonald's Ruth was telling me about her job interview.

She said she wants to be a dental assistant but didn't get the job.

"There are a lot of dentists," she said.

"But you'd be surprised how hard it is to find openings for dental assistants," she said.

DIKKERS

Today I went to my astronomy class.

Then I came home and ate a sandwich and watched some game shows.

Steve watched for a while too.

He guessed at the answers to the game shows' questions.

I tried to do some homework today.

But I didn't feel like it, so I took a walk outside.

I went to an ice cream store and bought a chocolate shake.

When I finally got home it was time for me to go to work at McDonald's.

Tony called his dad today.

"Leave me alone! This is a private conversation," he said.

His dad had a big operation and just got out of the hospital.

When Tony was done and sat by Steve and me, Mr. Peterson ran away really fast.

Today I heard Tony from the next room, "Jim, you gotta see this!"

When I looked, Mr. Peterson ran away really fast.

"You scared him!" Tony said.

Tony explained how Mr. Peterson was playing with Tony's shoelaces.

Today Tony got some barbecue mix to make a barbecue burger.

The mix made too much so he gave Steve and me some burgers.

When we were done eating, Tony said, "I cooked, so you guys get to do the dishes."

The bowl Tony used had a big orange stain in it that wouldn't come off.

Today in my Chinese history class we got our term papers back.

I got a C-.

I used to get higher grades by not working very hard.

I guess classes are getting harder.

A few days ago Tony won some movie tickets from a radio contest.

Today he said, "Hey, let's all go! This is our last week of school, let's celebrate!"

We went to the movie and it was pretty bad.

While we were walking home Tony said he didn't think it was that bad.

Today was the last day of classes for the semester.

It was a warm day and everybody wanted to be outside.

The professor ended class a little early and said, "Have a good summer."

Everybody put their books away and left in a hurry.